My mothe
She shared her genuine lo
She taught us the power of the w
She believed we have an int

Her philanthropic spirit was a
Literacy for Kids,
In honor of her selfless p
directly fund LFK's effor
With

Dinosaurs Living in MY HAIR! 3
An Underwater Adventure
by Jayne M Rose-Vallee
illustrated by Bonnie Helen Hawkins

Summer is here. It's the first week of camp.
Where adventure is part of each day.
My name is Espuardo and these are my friends.
Meet Gage, and Sabrina, and Faye!

We'll snorkel and kayak; we'll dive and we'll swim.
We'll learn about fishes and more.
The friendly camp dog slobbers kisses on us.
We laugh as we race for the shore.

The counselors teach us how things are connected.
The facts about reefs are so cool!
When we dive, our fish friends tell us all that they know.
This learning is better than school.

We discover our oceans need much better care
From people who live on the land.
The cry from marine life grows louder each day:
"Please clean up your waste from our sand."

Before you read further you might as well know,
The four of us share something weird.
Dinosaurs live in the curls on our head.
One day they just simply appeared!

Spinosaurus swims well, like a croc with no fear,
But for others the water is new.
We teach them to float, hold their breath, and be calm.
They love their face masks to peer through.

As we artfully slather on reef-safe sunscreen
Faye asks, "What if sharks lurk nearby?"
We think they are scary. T-Rex makes a face.
"Not to worry!" he says, "And here's why."

Spinosaurus explodes with a deep belly laugh.
He stretches his neck and remarks,
"One fact I can share which might lessen your angst;
I'm aquatic and *like* to eat sharks."

With fins on our feet and our dinosaurs prepped,
We fit our masks over our eyes.
We stomp to the surf and leave tracks as we go.
Above us a large osprey flies.

Beneath the blue surface, sea life is amazing.
So many new creatures live here.
The world is made up of more ocean than land.
It's fun to explore this frontier.

16

The hogfish is named for its pig-looking snout.
The grunt fish goes grunt when it eats.
The parrotfish, named for its parrot-like beak,
Poops sand, which is great for the beach.

That fish is a stunner with blues and bright yellow.
The queen triggerfish is a beauty.
She munches sea urchins, is fast and quite fierce,
But her mustache lines make her look snooty.

A doctorfish, trumpetfish, goatfish, and snapper,
All can be seen up ahead.
The goatfish has whiskers. The long one's the trumpet.
The snapper's the one that is red.

A seahorse is technically a tiny fish.
A rounded tail helps it hold on.
Although not fast swimmers, the one thing they do,
Is dance hooked together at dawn.

The ocean floor's sick from our plastic and trash.
For the coral, protection's a must.
Commit to save life in this watery world.
Its future depends upon us.

Just then without warning, a shadow appears.
A shark lingers off to our side.
Fish scatter and dart behind coral and rocks.
Some scoot in our ringlets and hide.

I hold very still. I am frightened a bit.
Spinosaurus is thinking "Mealtime!"
But that's when he sees an old fishing net's caught
Around the shark's belly and spine.

Spino's kindhearted, forgets about hunger.
He bites, chews and gnaws at the net.
It falls away slowly. The shark is now free.
Spinosaurus the hero? You bet!

Fish slip from our curls and pop out of hiding.
Relief shows in bubbles galore.
In glad celebration, we tumble and twirl.
The dinosaurs join with a *ROAR*.

As we clumsily wade through the water to shore,
Faye yells and then points to the sky.
The wind has picked up some old trash from the beach.
"We must stop it before it soars by!"

T-Rex nabs a chip bag. Gage snatches a straw.
I pick up old torn swimming briefs.
We head to the sand where we clean and we comb.
It's our job to protect our friends' reef.

Every day we are thoughtful about how we live.
We know it's important to *think*.
We help where we can. There is much to be done.
It's far better than going extinct!

Diving Deeper

How fast can an **OSPREY** fly? Around 80 MPH.

Over 1 million marine animals (including **SEA TURTLES**) are killed each year due to plastic debris in the ocean.

A **REEF** is a bar of rock, sand, coral, or other material lying beneath the surface of the water.

SEAHORSES can swim five feet in one hour.

QUEEN TRIGGERFISH can move each eye independently of the other.

PARROTFISH have teeth which are stronger than either gold, copper, or silver.

SHARKS have skin that feels like sandpaper.

True or False:

TRUMPETFISH can change colors.
True.
They change colors to blend in to their surroundings.
TRUMPETFISH are related to seahorses.
True.
Like seahorses, they are very poor swimmers.

HERMIT CRABS trap themselves in plastic waste. Things like straws, shoes, bottle caps, water bottles, and plastic bags cause them harm.

REEF-SAFE means it is not harmful to marine life in the reefs.

Link for more information

Dinosaurs Living in MY HAIR! 3

Published by Rosevallee Creations LLC

ROSEVALLEE
CREATIONS

First Edition 2022
ISBN 978-0-9861922-4-1

Library of Congress Control Number: 2021907942

Printed in USA on paper from responsible sources. Printed with UV inks.

For additional resources, video presentations, and educational information, please visit: Jaynerosevallee.com.

Jayne M
Rose-Vallee •

All monies raised through the DLIMH book series directly fund

literacy for kids.

a 501(c)(3) non-profit. To learn more, visit Literacyforkids.org.